PATRICK MAHOMES

SUPERSTAR QUARTERBACK

BIG BUDDY

★ NFL ★
SUPERSTARS

Big Buddy Books
An Imprint of Abdo Publishing
abdobooks.com

DENNIS ST. SAUVER

abdobooks.com

Published by Abdo Publishing, a division of ABDO, PO Box 398166, Minneapolis, Minnesota 55439.
Copyright © 2020 by Abdo Consulting Group, Inc. International copyrights reserved in all countries.
No part of this book may be reproduced in any form without written permission from the publisher.
Big Buddy Books™ is a trademark and logo of Abdo Publishing.

Printed in the United States of America, North Mankato, Minnesota.
052019
092019

THIS BOOK CONTAINS
RECYCLED MATERIALS

Cover Photo: efks/Getty Images; Harry How/Getty Images.
Interior Photos: Adam Glanzman/Getty Images (p. 5); Chelsea Purgahn/AP Images (p. 13); Colin
    Braley/AP Images (p. 25); David Eulitt/Getty Images (p. 19); Dustin Bradford/Getty Images (p.
    17); Jamie Squire/Getty Images (pp. 21, 23); Justin Edmonds/Getty Images (p. 27); Patrick Smith/
    Getty Images (p. 29); Peter Aiken/Getty Images (p. 15); Ronald Martinez/Getty Images (p. 9);
    Victor Texcucano/AP Images (p. 11).

Coordinating Series Editor: Elizabeth Andrews
Graphic Design: Jenny Christensen, Cody Laberda

Library of Congress Control Number: 2018967166

Publisher's Cataloging-in-Publication Data

Names: St. Sauver, Dennis, author.
Title: Patrick Mahomes: superstar quarterback / by Dennis St. Sauver
Other title: Superstar quarterback
Description: Minneapolis, Minnesota : Abdo Publishing, 2020 | Series: NFL superstars |
    Includes online resources and index.
Identifiers: ISBN 9781532119835 (lib. bdg.) | ISBN 9781532174599 (ebook)
Subjects: LCSH: Quarterbacks (Football)--United States--Biography--Juvenile literature. |
    Football players--United States--Biography--Juvenile literature. | Kansas City Chiefs
    (Football team)--Juvenile literature. | Sports--Biography--Juvenile literature.
Classification: DDC 796.3326409 [B]--dc23

CONTENTS

SUPERSTAR QUARTERBACK

Patrick Mahomes is a **professional** football player in the National Football League (NFL). He plays quarterback for the Kansas City Chiefs in Missouri. Many feel that he is what the Chiefs need to be **champions**.

SNAPSHOT

NAME:
Patrick Lavon
Mahomes II

BIRTHDAY:
September 17, 1995

BIRTHPLACE:
Tyler, Texas

POSITION:
Quarterback

COLLEGE TEAM:
Texas Tech University
Red Raiders

CURRENT TEAM:
Kansas City Chiefs

EARLY YEARS

Patrick's parents are Pat Mahomes and Randi Martin. Pat was a pitcher in Major League Baseball (MLB) who played for many different teams. Patrick has a younger brother Jackson, and a younger sister Mia.

Patrick's family is very close. His dad taught him about **professional** sports. His mom **encouraged** him when things got tough.

Where was Patrick Mahomes born?

CANADA

UNITED STATES OF
AMERICA

MEXICO

New
Mexico

Oklahoma

Arkansas

Tyler

Texas

Louisiana

MEXICO

Gulf of
Mexico

N

W   E

S

STARTING OUT

Like many athletes, Patrick liked to play sports as a kid. In high school, he played baseball, basketball, and football. In baseball, he was a star pitcher like his dad.

Patrick could have played **professional** baseball. The Detroit Tigers **drafted** him after high school. Patrick had to choose between baseball and football.

Patrick's dad Pat played in the MLB for 11 years. He played for six different teams during that time.

★ ★ ★ ★ ★ ★ ★ ★

Patrick was a three-star **prospect** in football. That meant that many college **scouts** wanted him to play for their schools. Patrick decided to play football at Texas Tech University.

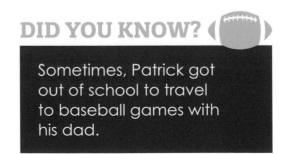

DID YOU KNOW?

Sometimes, Patrick got out of school to travel to baseball games with his dad.

Patrick said that he can throw a football between 80-85 yards (73-78 m). That is more than half the length of a football field!

BIG DREAMS

In his first two years of college, Patrick played in 20 total football games. He **passed** for 52 touchdowns and more than 6,000 yards (5,486 m).

In his third year, he set several records. Patrick passed for 734 yards (671 m) in one game. That tied the NCAA record for single-game passing yards.

Patrick decided to leave college to enter the 2017 NFL Draft.

GOING PRO

In 2017, the Kansas City Chiefs **drafted** Patrick. He was the tenth player picked. He did not play a lot in his first year. Instead, he spent time watching, learning, and waiting for his chance.

DID YOU KNOW?

Patrick said that he loves having a new challenge every week.

While trying out for the NFL draft, Patrick threw the football 60 miles (97 km) per hour!

★ ★ ★ ★ ★ ★ ★ ★

He played his first NFL game late in the 2017 season. He led the team to victory against the Denver Broncos with a score of 27-24. That day, he **passed** for 284 yards (260 m). It was a sign of exciting things to come.

Patrick became the starting quarterback in 2018. In his first game of the season, his team won against the Los Angeles Chargers. He threw for 256 yards (234 m) and had four touchdown passes.

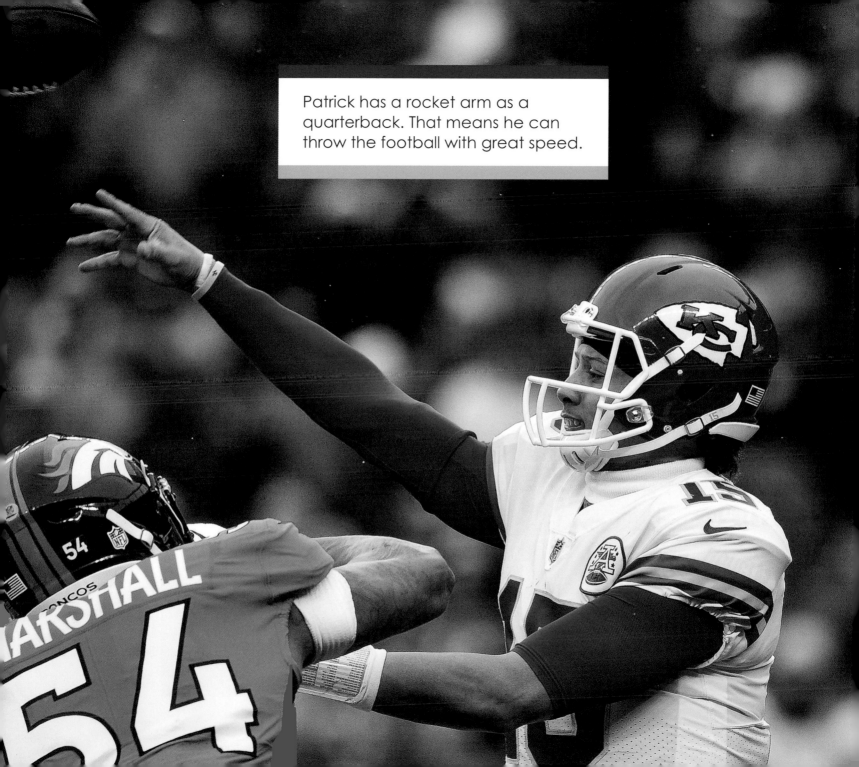

Patrick has a rocket arm as a quarterback. That means he can throw the football with great speed.

A RISING STAR

Only halfway through the 2018 season, Patrick broke the Chief's single-season record for touchdowns. He threw his thirty-first touchdown in a game against the Arizona Cardinals. The original record was set back in 1964.

DID YOU KNOW?

Patrick became the youngest player to throw six touchdowns in a single game. He was only 22 years old when he set that record!

In 2018, Patrick helped his team win the AFC West Division title.

Throughout the 2018 season, Patrick threw for four or more touchdowns seven times. In weeks two and 11, he threw for six touchdowns! He **passed** for 5,097 yards (4,661 m) and 50 touchdowns that year.

Patrick's dad gave his son the nickname Showtime.

OFF THE FIELD

When not playing football, Patrick enjoys spending time with his girlfriend Brittany. The two met when they were in high school. Brittany is also an athlete who loves playing soccer.

One of Patrick's hobbies is playing golf. He plays whenever he gets a chance. He also likes to travel. Patrick and Brittany visited Hawaii in June 2018.

Although he chose to play professional football, Patrick still enjoys watching baseball and basketball.

GIVING BACK

Being a star quarterback does not stop Patrick from caring for others. He has spent time at community centers in Kansas City. He has given gifts and food to children and their parents.

He also made time to visit kids who were in the hospital. He talked with them and even signed **autographs**.

NEED HELP ?

EVERY SEASON STARTS AT
DICK'S
SPORTING GOODS.

DATE _November 27, 2018_

PAY TO THE ORDER OF __KC UNITED__ $5,000

__Five-Thousand & 00/100__   DOLLARS

FOR __Sports Matter__   _DICK'S Sporting Goods_

Patrick works with the Sports Matter program by DICK'S Sporting Goods. In 2018, he presented $5,000 to a youth football group for the Sports Matter program.

AWARDS

While in college in 2016, Patrick won the Sammy Baugh Trophy. It is given each year to the top **passer** in the country.

Patrick was also a good student in college. He was named to the Academic **All-American** second team. He is only the second Texas Tech quarterback to earn that honor.

In September 2018, Patrick won back-to-back AFC Player of the Week awards. Later in the month, he was named AFC Offensive Player of the Month.

BUZZ

Patrick earned the AP **Most Valuable Player (MVP)** Award for the 2018 season. And he was the AFC starting quarterback in the **Pro Bowl** in January 2019.

The Chiefs will continue to have successful seasons while Patrick is on the team. Fans are excited to see what he does next!

In the 2018 AFC title game against the New England Patriots, Patrick threw for 295 yards (270 m)!

GLOSSARY

All-American selected as one of the best in the US in a particular sport.

autograph a person's signature written by hand.

champion the winner of a championship. A championship is a game, a match, or a race held to find a first-place winner.

draft a system for professional sports teams to choose new players.

encourage to make more determined, hopeful, or confident.

Most Valuable Player (MVP) the player who contributes the most to his or her team's success.

pass to throw the football in the direction of the opponent's goal.

Pro Bowl a game that features the best players in the NFL. It does not count toward regular-season records.

professional (pruh-FEHSH-nuhl) paid to do a sport or activity.

prospect someone or something that is likely to be successful.

scout a person whose job is to search for talented performers or athletes.

ONLINE RESOURCES

Booklinks
NONFICTION NETWORK
FREE! ONLINE NONFICTION RESOURCES

To learn more about Patrick Mahomes, please visit **abdobooklinks.com** or scan this QR code. These links are routinely monitored and updated to provide the most current information available.

★★★ INDEX ★★★